The Enlightened Ex-Offender

Corey Austin

This publication is designed to provide accurate and authoritative information with regard to the subject matter covered. It is sold with the understanding that neither the author nor the publisher is engaged in rendering legal, accounting, or other professional advice. If legal advice or other expert assistance is required, the services of a competent professional person should be sought.
--From a Declaration of Principles jointly adopted by a committee of the American Bar Association and a Committee of Publishers and Associations

Without limiting the rights under copyright reserved above, no part of this publication may be reproduced, transmitted, in any form, or by any means (electronic, mechanical, photocopying, recording, or otherwise), without the prior written consent of the copyright owner of this book.

*Bulk book discounts available

Copyright © 2014 Corey Austin
All rights reserved.

ISBN: 0692225838
ISBN 13: 9780692225837
Library of Congress Control Number: 2014909568
Corey Austin
Toledo, OH

TABLE OF CONTENTS

INTRODUCTION vii

CHAPTER 1 GETTING YOUR MIND RIGHT 1
    EVERYONE SUFFERS 1
    DOES EVIL REALLY EXIST IN THE WORLD? 2
    MANAGING FEAR 2
    STOPPING THE NEGATIVITY 3
    COOLING ANGER 3
    FINDING FORGIVENESS 4
    EMOTIONAL INTELLIGENCE 4
    HOW ENERGY AFFECTS YOU 5
    HOW LONG DOES IT TAKE TO HEAL? 5
    TAKE CONTROL OF YOUR EVERYDAY THOUGHTS 6
    RESPECT YOURSELF 6
    SHOULD YOU CARE WHAT PEOPLE THINK
    ABOUT YOU? 7
    HEALTHY RELATIONSHIPS 7
    RESTING YOUR MIND 10
    JOURNAL 12

CHAPTER 2 GETTING YOUR BODY RIGHT 22
    FIND THE BEST INFORMATION 22
    WHAT'S THE BEST MEDICINE? 23
    CHANGE UP YOUR ROUTINE 24
    PLACES TO START 25
    JOURNAL 35

CHAPTER 3 WHAT'S MISSING? 42
    SPIRITUALITY 42
    DECIDE YOUR OWN REALITY 43
    PLACES TO START 44
    JOURNAL 47

CHAPTER 4 FIGURING OUT ADDICTIONS 54
- DEFINITION 54
- ADDICTIONS USED AS MIND CONTOL? 55
- POSSIBLE CAUSES 56
- THE TREATMENT IS TREATING THE CAUSE! 57
- JOURNAL 58

CHAPTER 5 THE SHORT TERM PLAN 62
- MAKING YOUR LIST 62
- NAMING YOUR LIST 65
- WORK 65
- IMAGE 69
- SURROUNDING YOURSELF WELL 73
- LIFE'S CHALLENGES 74
- JOURNAL 77

CHAPTER 6 BREAKING FREE 88
- RECIDIVISM 88
- THE MOST IMPORTANT TIME TO MAKE IT THROUGH! 90
- THE PUBLIC'S OPINION OF EX-OFFENDERS 90
- SUCCESSFUL PROBATION/PAROLE TIPS 91
- JOURNAL 99

CHAPTER 7 THE LONG TERM PLAN 103
- EXPUNGEMENT 103
- CAREER GOALS 103
- GOING BACK TO SCHOOL 104
- FINANCIAL GOALS 105
- HEALTH GOALS 105
- MAKING YOUR OWN SPACE 106
- GOALS CHANGE OVER TIME 106
- JOURNAL 108

CHAPTER 8 CHANGING THE SYSYEM 113
- WHY IS THE WORLD THE WAY IT IS? 113
- THE REAL PROBLEMS 117
- WHAT CAN YOU DO ABOUT IT? 120
- THE BEAUTIFUL TRUTH 124
- JOURNAL 125

APPENDIX 133
    CLASSES/MEETINGS USING THE ENLIGHTENED
    EX-OFFENDER BOOK 133
    THE ENLIGHTENED EX-OFFENDER
    COMPLETION FORM 135

ABOUT THE AUTHOR 137

CHAPTER NOTES 139

INTRODUCTION

How do you start to move on from the long and horrible experience of imprisonment? Everyone has done something in their lifetime that is a crime, most just didn't get caught. But I did.

My name is Corey Austin. I was born and raised in Toledo, Ohio. When I was 21 I was sentenced and went to state prison. Being in prison wasn't exactly easy, to say the least, but getting out was a whole different kind of challenge. Finding a secure place to live and a job, quick enough to get on your feet, are what everyone talks about. But it is extremely hard to find and hang on to those things when you feel like everything is in chaos. This book is what I wish someone would have handed to me, as I walked out the door into "freedom".

Chapter 1

GETTING YOUR MIND RIGHT

The hardest thing in life to understand is yourself. Everyone struggles to keep themselves calm and happy with fear and negativity floating all around. Healing your mind is not only possible; it's just waiting for you to be ready. You can't change the past. It doesn't do you any good to think about how many times you've failed and it no longer matters anyways. Today and tomorrow are what counts because that's what you <u>can</u> change. The best way to live with your mistakes is not to keep them at all. Learn what you can from them and let them go. Allow yourself to move forward!

EVERYONE SUFFERS

You should never feel that you're alone in your pain. There is not one person who has ever lived who has not suffered. Some people choose to keep it hidden inside, but that doesn't mean it's not there just the same. Other people get so used to suffering that after a long time they don't feel complete without it. They even grow to enjoy the attention from it. Suffering doesn't have to be a part of your life at all. There is always another way. Like any other skill, finding the painless way of living takes time and practice to get really good at.

DOES EVIL REALLY EXIST IN THE WORLD?

People do evil things, but it doesn't mean that they are evil. It means that they were so lost and confused at the time that they did something horrible. Everyone has a dark side. Evil is a lack of anything good or positive. It does however have a purpose. It is a learning tool. Without the bad things in life, how would we appreciate the good things?

MANAGING FEAR

Fear can take over your life, and make you afraid of anything and everything, but only if you let it. Anxiety, guilt, depression, anger, shame, worry, dread, and frustration are all parts of fear. These feelings are all common things that are a part of being human. The trick is to never allow yourself to think that you are helpless in the face of them. All the feeling of fear is really doing is trying to protect you. To get rid of the feeling of fear immediately do the following every time:

- Allow yourself to feel the fear.
- Figure out what it's trying to protect you from.
- Thank it for this protection.
- It has now finished its job so you can let the feeling go and focus on positive things.

Getting Your Mind Right

Don't try to fight the feeling of fear, because you will just feel it more. Accept that it is simply a part of life that can be easily managed once you know how.

STOPPING THE NEGATIVITY

Negativity is expecting and seeing bad experiences everywhere. Disappointment and uncertainty are a normal part of life. Do you choose to focus on the good parts of life or complain about the bad parts? Your everyday happiness really comes down to how you answer this question.

COOLING ANGER

Getting angry is a response to the feeling of fear. When you feel powerless or helpless it doesn't help to try and take back control of the situation with intimidation and aggressiveness. This will just create more fear. Keep your cool. Step back for a minute and look at the situation. What is going to be the smartest move? When you feel angry the best thing to do is take some time to completely calm down before you show your reaction.

Another important thing to remember about anger is that some people like upsetting other people. They might think it's funny or are threatened by you. Whatever the reason, it always relates back to their own fears in some way. Don't let their problem become your problem. Get in the habit of not giving anyone the power to make you upset.

FINDING FORGIVENESS

It is a healthy valuable thing to forgive and to be forgiven. This includes you forgiving others, other people forgiving you, *and* you forgiving yourself. The majority of the time it's easier said than done. Forgiveness has to be heartfelt to be real. You really have to feel it. Pain often gets in the way. Once forgiveness is given or received it has the power to lift huge burdens off people's shoulders so that everyone can move on. Forgiveness is needed to heal.

EMOTIONAL INTELLIGENCE

Happiness is about how you feel about yourself and the world around you day to day. The key word here is *YOU*. It's all about how you feel because your emotions control your mood. To control your emotions you have to be very aware of what you're feeling all the time.

- For at least seven days, write down on a piece of paper what kind of mood you are in and every time it changes, all the way through the day.

Writing this down will help you see everything that changes you to a negative mood. Be 100% honest and clear with yourself. Don't hold anything back. Once you know exactly what all these things are, you can start working one by one on how to not let those things effect you anymore.

Getting Your Mind Right

HOW ENERGY AFFECTS YOU

Have you ever been around someone that's in a bad mood and it brings down your mood too? There are all kinds of energy that can affect your mood. Other people's moods are the most noticeable. The most important thing to remember is that you can't control other people. You can only control you. When you are in a situation that you can't really distance yourself from other people, like at work for example, do your best to keep to yourself. Stop your mind from thinking about them at all, and choose something else that's positive to focus on. Other times, things like TV, music, or even a bunch of different background noises all at once are the problem. They can make you feel drained without even realizing how it happened. In any case, it's all about surrounding yourself with positive peaceful settings, and a lot of the time you might have to create this place for yourself in your own mind.

HOW LONG DOES IT TAKE TO HEAL?

Healing is a lifelong thing. There are always new hurts to get over and problems to overcome. You might feel better in one way, while you still have work to do in other areas. Here are some helpful tips to keep in mind:

- You can't heal all the way if you don't let go of the fear and negativity you hold inside.
- Never be so lost in your own hurt that you forget to treat the people around you well.
- Everyone feels a little emptiness from time to time, just remember to fill it up with positive things.

- You have to understand something before you can heal from it.
- Focus on what you love and appreciate.
- Let yourself feel excited about all the great things that will come along with feeling better.

TAKE CONTROL OF YOUR EVERYDAY THOUGHTS

Every thought that goes through your mind each day is equally if not more important than what you say out loud. Thoughts are things. They have a ton of power and influence on the present and your future. You need to train your mind to work for you and not against you. Never put yourself down. Stop using words like can't and won't. Give yourself credit when you do something good and remember your successes every day. Don't allow negativity in! Be able to see the good and bad things, planning for both, but choose to keep your thoughts focused on the good things!

RESPECT YOURSELF

If you're looking for a change, look at yourself first. Being locked up is dehumanizing. It's easy to lose yourself. The secret to finding yourself again or even for the first time is simple. Respect yourself. Ask yourself these seven questions:

1. Do you love yourself?
2. What will you not compromise about?
3. Are you nice to yourself?
4. Do you act confident?

5. What is most important to you?
6. Do you let anyone else think for or make decisions for you?
7. What would you change about yourself if you could?

Write down what you need to work on based on the list above. Do at least one thing a day to improve your list. If you write down everything you do, you will be able to see how far you've come in the future.

SHOULD YOU CARE WHAT PEOPLE THINK ABOUT YOU?

It does matter what other people think about you. Other people decide how to treat you based on how they feel about you. Make as good of an impression as you can on everyone you come across every day. Don't let it bother you if they decide that they don't like you, and not everyone will. Don't let it upset you. Think of people's opinion of you as a mirror of what kind of person they are. Some people you could sit down and tell your entire life story to and it wouldn't do anything to change their mind. That says something about them, not you. Work hard to be the best that you can be at all times and expect good things.

HEALTHY RELATIONSHIPS

After you have worked on yourself for long enough, you will know that even if you slide back a little you will always be able to get yourself back on track. At that point you can begin to think about improving your relationships with other people.

The Enlightened Ex-Offender

What every healthy relationship has in common

- Feeling understood
- Choosing compassion over brutal honesty
- Mutual trust
- Open communication
- Focusing on what you have in common
- Releasing the need to be critical, judgmental or controlling
- Being a good listener
- Giving and accepting the feeling of love openly
- Respecting other people's feelings and expecting people to respect yours
- Being assertive when needed
- Stating what your needs are
- Looking at things from the other persons point of view
- Equally balancing all the relationships of your life at the same time
- Showing appreciation for people
- Reducing the drama in your life down to as little as possible
- Never assuming you know what someone is thinking or feeing
- Admitting mistakes when you're wrong
- Understanding that any abuse, in any kind of relationship, is unacceptable
- Being able to let a relationship go when it's not healthy

Getting Your Mind Right

Family

You don't get to choose the family that you're born into, or the children that you bring into the world. The best that you can do is to work with what you are given. In most cases, effort on your part, patience, and time will get your relationship on a healthy track. There are some times however, that no matter how hard you try it doesn't seem to be making things any better. After so long it is okay to protect yourself by letting yourself be detached from someone. It doesn't mean that you have to cut them out of your life completely, just that you choose not to let yourself get upset when it comes to them.

Friends

Friends you do get to pick and choose. The most important thing to think about when deciding to let go of or keep a friend is this: Does this person have a positive or a negative influence on your life? It really is that simple. People are either supportive, accepting, and helpful or they're not.

Significant Others

Relationships that go past the normal limits of friendship and enter into the area of significant others can get really tricky. Here are some helpful tips:
- Make sure you want the same things in the future.
- Think about whether being together makes you both better people.
- There is no one kind of relationship that will work for everyone.

The Enlightened Ex-Offender

- Break unhealthy dating habits and types.
- Consider if your behavior needs to be more confident or more passive, etc.
- Don't be in a rush to get into a long term commitment.
- Any kind of abuse is not okay.
- The best way to handle an argument is to stop and wait until everyone is calm to talk about it.
- Ending a relationship is almost always messy, so try to sidestep drama wherever possible.
- Know that you can overcome most anything negative that happens to you because of a relationship.

RESTING YOUR MIND

By resting your mind you allow it to unclutter and refresh itself. There is no one thing that will work for everyone. Try a little bit of all of these and keep what works for you.

- Meditate
- Walk outdoors
- Keep a journal to write in
- Listen to positive music
- Read a helpful book
- Work out
- Practice yoga
- Take a short refresher nap
- Paint or draw
- Turn off the TV
- Take a long soothing bath
- Surround yourself with calming colors
- Take a well-planned-out day for yourself

Getting Your Mind Right

- Do something to make yourself laugh
- Light a scented candle
- Practice slow deep breathing

Keeping your mind calm and balanced should be part of your everyday routine. Nobody is perfect. You're not going to wake up one day and never have a negative moment again. It's not about being perfect, it's about learning and growing a little more each day.

Journal

Fear and Negativity
Practice handling your fear in this new way:
What is something that you presently fear?

_____

Close your eyes and allow yourself to feel it fully. What is it trying to protect you from?

_____

To yourself or out loud say "Thank you for your protection." Now that you have figured out why the fear was there and acknowledged it, you can let it go! What is a positive thought that you can put in place of it?

_____

Anytime you feel a fear pulling you down use this new process.

You can deal with <u>anger</u> in the same exact way that you deal with fear:

What is something that you get angry about?

_____

Getting Your Mind Right

Close your eyes and allow yourself to feel it fully. What is it trying to protect you from?

_____

To yourself or out loud say "Thank you for your protection." Now that you have figured out why the anger was there and acknowledged it, you can let it go! What is a positive thought that you can put in place of it?

_____

This processes works not only on fear and anger but any negative emotion because any negative emotion when you break it down is just a reaction to fear.

Another way of dealing with negativity.....
What are three things in your life that you complain about a lot?

1. _____

2. _____

3. _____

The Enlightened Ex-Offender

What are three positive things you can focus on in place of those three things?

1. _____

2. _____

3. _____

Taking a negative thought and turning it into a positive one might seem too simple to be the key to success and happiness, but you will notice that the people who say that are not very successful or happy.

Finding Forgiveness

What are three things that you would feel a weight off of your shoulders if you could forgive?

1. _____

2. _____

3. _____

Getting Your Mind Right

A deep understanding of a situation/person is needed before you can start to forgive. What could you learn more about to understand what happened better? Why was this situation the way it was?

_____

_____

Emotional Intelligence

As mentioned in this chapter topic, for at least seven days write down on a piece of paper what kind of mood you are in and every time it changes, all the way through the day.

Day1 _____

Day2 _____

Day3 _____

Day4 _____

Day5 _____

Day6 _____

Day7 _____

The Enlightened Ex-Offender

What happened to put you in good moods?

___

What put you in bad moods?

___

What changes could you make to have more good moods and less bad moods?

___

How Energy Affects You

Where do you feel good energy? Is it the place, the people there or both?

___

Where do you feel negative energy? Is it the place, the people there or both?

___

How can you spend more of your time around the good energy?

___

Getting Your Mind Right

How Long Does It Take to Heal?

Healing starts to come in the same way that forgiveness does with understanding.

What are three things about yourself that need to heal?

1. _____

2. _____

3. _____

How will you start this process?

_____

What are three things about your relationship with others that need to heal?

1. _____

2. _____

3. _____

How will you start this process?

_____

The Enlightened Ex-Offender

Take Control of Your Every Day Thoughts

How many of your thoughts in a day are positive and how many are negative? You have thousands of thoughts a day so just try to get a good estimate. Take at least a full day to reflect to answer this question.

_____

Where is there room for improvement?

_____

Mark on your calendar in a month to ask yourself this question again. How do you feel different?

_____

Respect Yourself

Using the list of seven question from chapter one under the Resect Yourself chapter topic, what do you think would make you feel better to work on?

_____

_____

_____

Getting Your Mind Right

Actively do at least one thing a day to improve towards your goals! What will you do today?

_____

Healthy Relationships

This might sound a bit selfish but you need a plan, ahead of time, to figure out what relationships (family, friends and significant others) that you are going to put your full attention and effort into and what ones you are going to gently let go. Obviously, you only want to keep the ones that are healthy for your mind, body and soul. These might be very hard decisions. How much focus and attention you are going to give a healthy relationship is also a decision you need to make because you only have so much time and energy to go around. Write down every important person in your life. (Use code names and be careful exactly how you write things so people won't be able to tell who you're writing about if they happen to read it.) Figure out what you want the future of that healthy relationship to be and what you're going to do to get it there. (Use the Healthy Relationships chapter topic to help you.)

_____

_____

_____

The Enlightened Ex-Offender

_____

_____

_____

Resting Your Mind

Give each suggestion under resting your mind a try at least once. There is no way to tell what will work for you until you try it. You might be surprised! What are the first three you want to try?

_____

_____

_____

Getting Your Mind Right

Other Notes:

Chapter 2

GETTING YOUR BODY RIGHT

How your body feels day to day effects every part of your life. People usually don't realize how important being in good health is until they're not anymore. It's never too late to start taking better care of yourself again or even for the first time.

FIND THE BEST INFORMATION

There are millions of people and places telling you how to take the best care of yourself. A lot of these places are more interested in how much money they can make from you than if what they are selling is really what's best for you. Money clouds the health industry's judgment just as much as anyone else's. The real best way to take care of yourself is to get as much information as you can and decide what works for you.

- Get expert opinions including traditionally accepted as well as alternative ones.
- Ask the right people for their opinion. (A.k.a. don't ask your mechanic how to bake a cake and don't ask your bakery how to fix a car.)

- Look it up on the internet from different points of view.
- Don't ever trust just one or two opinions, get a whole bunch.

WHAT'S THE BEST MEDICINE?

Western Medicine is the treatment of medical conditions with medications, by doctors, nurses and other similar healthcare specialists using western medical and scientific traditions.
- The best option for emergency health care right now.
- Medicines that doctors prescribe don't always make us healthier and can also become addicting. Only take a medication if the benefit is worth the risk.[1]
- More than half of graduating doctors admit they don't know enough about nutrition to give advice about it. Healthy nutrition can prevent having many medical emergencies in the first place.

Eastern Medicine includes medical practices from the countries that make up Asia.
- A few examples are acupuncture, martial arts, herbal medicine, Feng Shui and massage.
- Eastern medicine relies more on the observations of the practitioner than on machines to diagnose.
- How a person's mind and "spirit" are feeling are also taken into account for a physical diagnosis.

Alternative Medicines are healing skills not taught in traditional Western medical schools.

- These include Eastern medicine and many more such as Australasia & Oceania, Mediterranean & Near Eastern, African, and the Americas.
- Complimentary medicine means you are using an alternative medicine with western medicine, not just an alternative one by itself.

So which one should you use? All of them! Take what works for you from every kind of medicine there is. As long as you're doing your research along the way to make sure that it's safe for you, there's more than one place you can look to get and keep healthy.

CHANGE UP YOUR ROUTINE

You can have all the best intentions and greatest information in the world, but all that won't matter if you can't figure out how to get yourself in the habit of doing all these great things.

- There is no exact amount of days that it takes to make or break a habit. It's a little different for everyone.
- 30 days is a good place to start, but getting out of bad habits and into good ones is a lifelong thing.
- It's easier to make a habit than to break one, and even the most disciplined people get into bad habits once in a while.
- The best way to change a habit is to have a new one ready to replace the old one.
- Your new habit should be a well thought out health goal you have set for yourself.[2,3]

Getting Your Body Right

- If you're having extreme difficulty changing a habit, ask yourself what emotion or fear is holding you back and then decide on a healthier way to go forward.

There are so many different things to think about that it may seem impossible to change them all. Get organized and plan all of your changes out before you get started. Make sure that a habit that you haven't changed yet isn't sabotaging the current one you are trying to change. The order that you change things in can be very important, too.

PLACES TO START
1
Get Enough Sleep

The very first thing to work on is to get between seven and eight hours of sleep a night. Any more or less sleep will have unhealthy effects on an adult body.[4] The kind of sleep you get, being able to fall asleep on time, and how you feel when you wake up are also very important.

- Try to plan your schedule so that you can go to bed and get up at the same time every day.
- Make sure the temperature is cool, the room is dark, and the noise level is low.
- Avoid eating or drinking too much and any kind of stimulants.
- If you have to take a nap, try to limit it to a half an hour and in the mid afternoon.

- Make your bed as comfortable as possible.
- Create a routine at the end of the night for your body to get used to.
- Try a sleep promoting tea if you are still having problems.[5]

2
Eat To Feel Good

What you eat controls how much energy you have and what kind of mood you are in. Make it a priority to eat as healthy as you can.

- Try to eat so that you are keeping your body evenly energized at all times.
- Pay attention to portion sizes.
- Read the nutritional facts for everything that you eat and drink, and know what amounts you are aiming for.
- What you eat is just as important as how much you eat.
- Make sure you are getting enough vitamins and minerals.
- Eat foods that are in season.
- Consult a nutritionist or certified health coach when you can for extra advice.
- Start thinking of food as medicine instead of a pleasure source.
- Eat as financially healthy as you can afford to. It really is a great investment that will pay for itself in the future.

Getting Your Body Right

Take the time to learn everything you can about nutrition. There is a lot to know and new discoveries are always being made on what is healthiest for the human body. Keep up to date on the latest information!

3
A Healthy Body Weight

Getting and keeping a healthy body weight is another thing that you will spend your lifetime working on. It can seem more complicated than it really is to gain or lose weight, so focus your attention on the basics.

What is a healthy body weight?

To decide a starting goal for how much you should weigh, find your BMI or look on a height weight data chart. People have different body types so a healthy body weight will be a little different from person to person.

The healthy way to lose weight

- Try to eat slightly less calories than are recommended in a day or burn off calories to get to a little less, or both. (But remember there is a whole lot more to it than just that!)
- What you eat, what time of day or night you eat it and with what other foods you eat it with all have huge effects on weight.
- Never go on a diet ever again. Change your habits for what and how you eat for the rest of your life.

- Focus your thoughts on what a food will do for your body instead of focusing on the temporary pleasure it will give you.
- Get a food allergy test to see if there are any foods that are unknowingly causing a problem, or if you can't afford one try taking certain foods out of your diet temporarily to see what effect it has on your body.

4
Drink A Lot Of Water

An average adult's body weight is 50-70 percent water.[6] When you drink water you are replacing the water that you naturally loose in a day so you don't get dehydrated. You need to replace water with water. Think of it this way; would you take a bath in soda pop every day for the rest of your life? Then why is it okay to fill the inside of your body with it?

What does water do for you?

It keeps your body temperature normal, lubricates and cushions your joints, helps protect sensitive tissues, and gets rid of waste.

Do we get water from other places besides drinking it?

We also get some water from other drinks and solid foods like fruit.

Getting Your Body Right

How much water do we need a day?
Most adults need 6-8 medium sized glasses of water a day. The more extra physical activity you do in a day the more extra water you will need.

Is bottled water better?
There are many different opinions on what is safe and unsafe water. Some people will only drink water that has been purified through reverse osmosis filters in non-plastic containers because they say that anything else is toxic and poisoning you. This is a good one to look up and research yourself to decide what you think.

What are a couple good tips to get into the habit of drinking more water?
Always carry a bottle (or glass bottle) of water around with you and add a slice of fruit in it if you want some extra flavor.[7]

There is a theory in the book "The True Power of Water" by Masaru Emoto that the quality of water changes according to the message we give it or how we feel about it. This sounds kind of crazy at first, but if we are over half water ourselves, it's not so crazy to think that we might have some connection to it. Whether this is something you're open to or not, it certainly can't hurt to send some positive vibes of love and appreciation out to the water you drink.[8]

5
Exercise On A Regular Basis

Exercise is just as important for your body as sleep or food. Every morning take a quick walk to get your body awake and moving, and stretch before going to bed. Don't exercise intensely every day. Warm up for at least 5 minutes before starting a workout. Beginners should start out slow at three days a week and even the most in shape people shouldn't exercise for more than 60 minutes a day or more than 200 minutes total a week. Weight training should be done no more than three times a week on the same muscles and never done two days in a row.[9] Include some core stability and balance training in your workout too.[10] End with 5-10 minutes of stretches targeting the main muscle groups.

Why should you put all that effort into exercising?

- Not being active is just as unhealthy as smoking.
- Increases strength and endurance.
- Reduces stress, the chance of injury, heart disease, high blood pressure, cancer, diabetes and other diseases.
- Improves appearance, mood, posture, flexibility, balance, and coordination.
- Helps your body to use less energy on a regular basis, relaxes muscles, controls body weight, sleep is better, delays the ageing process and to look and feel younger.

Getting Your Body Right

If finding the time to exercise is a problem, plan your week out ahead of time to make sure you fit it in. Design a workout routine, set goals, and keep track of your progress. Change up your exercise routine every so often to get the best results for your effort. Exercising doesn't have to be expensive. Working out at home can be just as effective as a gym. Don't let anything keep you from looking and feeling your best! [9,10]

6
Protect Against Toxins

Toxins are anything that shouldn't be in your system such as residue leftover from things like medications, food and your environment. Detoxing is when someone uses colonics, powders, and drinkable or herbal cleanses to get rid of the toxins in their body. Opinions on detoxifying your body are mixed. Lots of people swear by its positive effects, but some doctors warn that it can actually have harmful effects.[11] This is a subject that is definitely worth looking into more to see what feels right for you. In the meantime some agreed on simple ways of avoiding toxins are:

- Wipe your shoes on a good door matt or take them off before going indoors.
- Try to avoid plastic shower curtains and mattress covers made with PVC.
- Wash your fruit and vegetables from top to bottom with water
- Choose fresh air over air fresheners[12]

7
Listen To What Your Body Is Telling You

One of the best ways to prevent future health problems is to start listening to what your body is telling you today. Most major chronic conditions can be prevented.

- Note any feeling of pain.
- Be aware of any changes in things like your nails, tongue, hair, bowel movements, eye lids, urine, body temperature etc.
- Try to plan regular checkups with a family doctor and dentist.
- Take extra good care of your body when it's sick even if medicine is hiding your symptoms.
- Keep the correct body posture.
- Practice self-exams on a regular basis.
- Don't ever hurt your body to look good.
- Slow down and let your body rest when it is tired.[13],[14]

There are also some specific health concerns, that people recently released from prison, should be aware of. At the time of release, two thirds of women and half of men have been diagnosed with a chronic physical health condition. The most common conditions were asthma, hepatitis infection, high blood pressure, arthritis, high cholesterol and back pain.[15]

Listen to and trust your body. When something out of the ordinary happens write it down with the date and time of its occurrence. Keep all of the notes in one place so you'll have them handy when you next see a doctor, nutritionist, health coach, etc.

8
How You Feel About Your Body Is Important

Media and marketing experts want you to feel insecure so that you will buy things to make yourself feel better. Remember this fact when you are watching TV, looking at a billboard, reading a magazine, or anything like that. Everyone struggles with loving their bodies and yes there are always things that you can improve. But regardless of where you are in your life, you have to love yourself at all times. When you do, you will naturally take better care of your body.

9
Tips For Aging Well

Everyone hopes that they will be a perfect example of good health when they grow old. Taking care of yourself throughout your life is the most important thing you can do to age well. If you haven't taken very good care of yourself up until now, don't beat yourself up about it, just start taking care of yourself from now on as best you can.

The field of anti-aging medicine is working on discovering how to slow down or reverse the ageing process all together. Some scientists believe that eventually we will have the technology to keep the human body living forever!

There are a ton of anti-aging products on the market that haven't been proven to work yet, so be careful that you're not wasting your money. That being said, there are also many things that do work, especially ones that will increase the quality of your life. Here are more ways to increase/keep the quality of your life:

- Keep your brain active and always learning something new.
- Choose to be a positive happy person. (They live better and longer).
- Hormone replacement therapy is growing in popularity, and worth looking into if/when your budget can afford it.
- Stay a connected active participant in the world by caring and contributing to the bigger picture, not just yourself.

Don't be afraid to make aging well one of your top priorities. You'll thank yourself later!

Put all your focus, thoughts and attention into your health goals until what you're working on becomes a habit. Put up visual reminders, set a message on your phone alarm, email yourself, etc. Everyone is a little different. It's all about finding what works and makes you feel your best!

Journal

Change Up Your Routine
What is a habit that you would like to break?

_____

What fear is this habit trying to protect you from?

_____

Acknowledge, thank and release this fear. What positive habit are you going to replace it with?

_____

_____

Are there any habits that you need to change first so that they do not interfere with one you are trying to change now?

_____

_____

The Enlightened Ex-Offender

Get Enough Sleep
What is your idea of a perfect sleeping environment?

_____

_____

What can you do to get it closer to your ideal now and in the future?

_____

_____

Eat To Feel Good
What are the three most important things about your eating you want to focus on for you?

1. _____

2. _____

3. _____

A Healthy Body Weight
What is your ideal body weight?

_____

Getting Your Body Right

What are three things that you want to focus on to get/keep it there?

1. _____

2. _____

3. _____

Drink A Lot Of Water
How much water do you drink a day?

_____

How can you make it so you can drink more?

_____

_____

Exercise On A Regular Basis
What are your exercise goals?

_____

_____

The Enlightened Ex-Offender

What are you going to do to make sure you achieve them?

_____

_____

Protect Against Toxins

What are three ways that you can start eliminating toxins out of your life?

1. _____

2. _____

3. _____

Listen To What Your Body Is Telling You

What is one thing that your body is trying to tell you right now?

_____

_____

How can you listen better in the future?

_____

_____

Getting Your Body Right

How You Feel About Your Body Is Important

How do you feel about your body? (In detail)

_____

_____

_____

_____

Are you more focused on being truly healthy or on the image that the media gives you to aspire to?

_____

_____

What do you want your body to be like in the future?

_____

_____

The Enlightened Ex-Offender

List three things that you can do now towards achieving that goal:

1. _____

2. _____

3. _____

Tips For Aging Well

What are you going to do now, for your body and mind, that will help you age well in the future?

_____

_____

_____

_____

Getting Your Body Right

Notes:

Chapter 3

WHAT'S MISSING?

Your beliefs, attitudes, and how you feel about the world will determine how far you get in life. It's a fact that a positive outlook on life will make you more successful. Being positive is a choice people make a thousand times a day. It takes practice because it's easier to be negative. Search with an open heart and mind for the things in life that feel right. There are many different paths you could choose to take. The most important thing is that you keep moving down the path, keep searching. Never settle for something you don't understand or that doesn't feel right to you. Don't look for someone else to give you your answers, find them for yourself. Your own personal truth cannot be found by anyone else. Find your truth.

SPIRITUALITY

The definition of spirituality is interest or concern for things of the spirit. Some people would say that the spirit and the soul are not the same thing, but we will use the word spirituality to mean exploring the part of you that, most agree, survives death.

It's not wrong to not know what you believe, but if you don't, you should be searching for your answers every day. Your

What's Missing?

heart suffers when you do not know your soul. A sense of peace comes with making sense of yourself and the world around you, and there is always something new to learn. It also helps to first think in terms of how things effect the whole world when you're thinking about something (remembering that this includes you because you are a part of this world), not just of how it effects you only. This will help you get a bigger picture. For example, the Iroquois people are said to work for the benefit of the seventh generation in the future.

Spirituality is often a very personal thing. If you don't want to share your beliefs with other people, that's okay, you don't have to. What you find should make you feel calm and connected, never fearful.

What's the difference between religion and spirituality?

Most religion is a specific path to take and spirituality can be any one you choose.

DECIDE YOUR OWN REALITY

You have more control over what happens in life than you think. Whatever you focus on you draw to you. "Focusing on" can mean intentionally or unintentionally. You will just as easily draw something you fear to you as you will something you love. Your thoughts control everything. Some people call this the law of attraction, the power of positive thinking, or mind over matter. The important thing is not what you call it, but that you use it!

What can this do for you on a daily basis?

You can choose how you want your life to feel. Feel it as if it's already how you want it and you will draw it to you. Think about what you want all the time and about how you are going to get it. How will it feel when you do? Practice controlling your thoughts and choose something healthy and positive for yourself.

Tips for mastering your everyday thoughts

- Speak to yourself nicely
- Use positive statements, words and sounds. Repeat them in your mind as often as you need to keep them there.
- Take the words can't and won't out of your thoughts completely

Be careful of expecting anything too specific. The goal is to feel a certain way. There are many ways to get to where you want to be.

PLACES TO START

Take a few days to think and focus on each one of these before you go on to another. Journal what you learn to go back to and read from time to time.

- Get to know yourself.
    - What are your strengths and weaknesses? Strong likes and dislikes? Loves and fears?

What's Missing?

- Be able to enjoy and be happy spending time with yourself.
- What do you feel is your purpose in life?
  - Could it be different at different times, or has it always been the same? Or both?
- Practice spirituality with your mind through meditation, affirmations and mantras.
  - If you don't know how, teach yourself. There are thousands of books and videos out there that explain how.
- Practice spirituality with your body through yoga or martial arts.
- Practice your spirituality through your soul by a chosen form of prayer.
- Learn about how everything is connected.
  - Science calls it sting theory and others call it the law of oneness, but whatever you call it, this will completely change how you see <u>everything</u>!
- Consider Altruism
  - The service of ones fellow man. Dedicate your life to something. Caring for people is just as important as breathing to the soul.
- Practice non-judgment
  - Controlling your thoughts to not form judgments but to accept and then move on to other thoughts.
- Talk to like-minded people for encouragement and feedback.

The Enlightened Ex-Offender

- Surround yourself with positive reminders of your new direction.
- Explore others' ideas, religions, and philosophies to help you figure out what feels right to you.
- Trust yourself to know what feels right for you.
- Take and use what works, and leave the rest.

Spiritually learning and growing takes time. It's something that you will continue to do for the rest of your life. The question is how fast do you want to grow and what direction do you want to take? The answer is a little different for everyone.

What's Missing?

Journal

SPIRITUALITY

Do your beliefs make you feel calm and connected with yourself and the things that surround you?

_____

What positive effects do your beliefs have on yourself and the world?

_____

DECIDE YOUR OWN REALITY

What are five things that your thoughts are focused on throughout your day?

1. _____

2. _____

3. _____

4. _____

5. _____

The Enlightened Ex-Offender

What five things would you ideally like your thoughts to be focused on through your day?

1. _____

2. _____

3. _____

4. _____

5. _____

What is your plan to work on getting your thoughts closer to what you want them to be?

_____

_____

_____

How do you want your life to feel? (In detail)

_____

_____

_____

What's Missing?

Try to feel everyday how you described above. Some days might be better than others, but with practice you really can control your own happiness and naturally will be surrounded more and more with the things that make you happy!

PLACES TO START
Get to know yourself better:
What are your strengths and weaknesses?

_____

_____

What are your strong likes and dislikes?

_____

_____

What do you strongly love and fear?

_____

_____

The Enlightened Ex-Offender

Are you happy and able to enjoy spending time by yourself?

_____

_____

What do you feel is your purpose in life?

_____

_____

Could it be different at different times, or has it always been the same? Or both?

_____

_____

Are you open to trying meditation, affirmations and mantras?

_____

Do you believe that everything is connected?

_____

What's Missing?

How good are you at controlling your thoughts to not form any sort of judgments about yourself or other people?

_____

_____

Do the people that you surround yourself with understand the power of controlling your thoughts/ happiness?

_____

_____

Does your personal space at home have reminders of your goals?

_____

What could you do to mentally improve your personal surroundings?

_____

_____

The Enlightened Ex-Offender

Are you open to others' viewpoints to see if there is anything you can learn from them?

_____

_____

What are three things that you want to learn more about so that you can learn more about yourself?

1. _____

2. _____

3. _____

What's Missing?

Notes:

Chapter 4

FIGURING OUT ADDICTIONS

Knowing what needs to be done and being able to do it on a regular basis are two very different things. Why is it so hard to change habits? You have to start by being healthy in your mind, body and soul (the first three chapters of this book), to be ready to figure out and change your addictions in a lasting way. Addictions are the symptoms of what's wrong on the inside of you, of your discontent and unhappiness. Those are the things that will trip you up back into an addiction over and over again. Once you feel like you have a strong foundation, you're ready to start tackling your addictions.

DEFINITION

An addiction is a persistent, compulsive dependence on a behavior or substance. There are two types of addictions; substance (example: drug) and process (example: gambling) addictions. Many people are addicted to more than one substance or process. Addictions will increase in severity over time if not treated. Anything taken to an extreme can become an addiction.[1]

Figuring Out Addictions

Examples of Common Addictions
- Tobacco
- Alcohol
- Illegal drugs
- Prescription drugs
- Lifestyle (friends, environment, neighborhood, etc.)
- Relationships
- TV, entertainments (The average American youth spends more time watching TV than they spend at school a year.)
- Food
- Shopping
- Attention
- Sex
- Gambling
- Caffeine
- Hoarding
- Work

Once you recognize and decide to start working on areas that you are having a problem with, the very first thing you should do is learn everything you can about it. What fear or anxiety are you trying to control with it? The more you understand a problem, the closer you are to overcoming it.

ADDICTIONS USED AS MIND CONTOL?

Fact: Someone is making money off of your addiction. Someone is using addiction to control your mind so that they can make a profit off it. From drug dealers and pharmaceutical companies to fast food restaurants and major TV stations, manipulation is coming from somewhere. Just one more reason to work on correcting an addiction.

POSSIBLE CAUSES

What causes/contributes to an addiction depends on who you ask. These are some of the top theories:

Changes in the Brain

Drug use over a long period of time can change the brain in important and possibly permanent ways. There are some changes that may be irreversible, especially emotional memories, related to drug use. But just as people with strokes are able to, addicts can recover by using other parts of their brain that weren't affected by the drugs.

Genetic Factors

It's becoming clear that substance abuse and addiction probably involve a genetic component. Inherited biological differences make some individuals either more or less at risk to drug dependency than others, but a genetic component by itself is not enough to produce substance abuse and addiction.

Psychological Factors

These factors include personality and presence of psychiatric disorders, as well as peer, family, and other environmental influences.

Figuring Out Addictions

Energy

Addiction is also said to be caused by imbalances in energy flow through the body. This can mean that there is too much of an energy, not enough of an energy, or none at all where there needs to be, affecting organs and systems throughout the body and causing an extreme of addiction.

THE TREATMENT IS TREATING THE CAUSE!

The cause of addiction is something that is critically important. It has to be searched for, brought out, sorted out totally, and healed before a person can hope to move on from it. Find the cause and then find a different better way to deal with what you have found.

When you are feeling clear minded, really look closely at your own feelings, thoughts, and motives. Personalize how to fix the root of the problem. There will probably be more than one root. A combination of causes may need a combination of changes to get things to where you need them to be. Keep searching for as long as it takes to find new healthier ways of doing things that works for you. Every part of you (mind, body and soul) must be deeply searched and healed with love, compassion, and tolerance that you give to yourself and others. <u>Everyone</u> falls down, just don't ever stop fighting to get back up!

Journal

What are the three things that you are most addicted to?

1. _____

2. _____

3. _____

How are these three addictions related to each other?

_____

_____

Are there any other addictions from the list of common addictions that contribute to your top three addictions?

_____

_____

What fears/anxieties are you trying to control with your addictions?

_____

_____

Figuring Out Addictions

_____

_____

What can you now do to make yourself feel better about the fear/anxiety that is driving the addiction? Plan out multiple healthy ways to make yourself feel better about each fear/anxiety. Start with the top three:

1. _____

2. _____

3. _____

_____

Dealing with an addiction takes time, usually a lot of time. The root of the fear and anxiety you find is sometimes so deep that you need help to think clearly to get past it. This is nothing to be ashamed of. There is not a single person on this earth that doesn't have some deep dark issue that they wouldn't need help to deal with. The most important thing is that you make a commitment to yourself to keep working on your fears/anxieties/addictions over time.

The Enlightened Ex-Offender

Write down that promise to yourself now:

_____

_____

_____

_____

Figuring Out Addictions

Notes:

Chapter 5

THE SHORT TERM PLAN

If you are at a point in your life where you need to change a lot of things, don't just throw everything out the window and start all over. Stop, take some time, and write it all out. Write down the things in your life that you want to keep. These are the things that are positive, working for you and will continue to work for you. Then write down the things in your life that you want to change. Some things you will be able to change without much effort right away. Other things might need a plan with good timing to be changed. Start with making a to-do list and just do as the old saying goes; Plan your work and work your plan.

MAKING YOUR LIST
Goals

Where do you want to be in your life in a year? In three years? In five years? Goals help make your plan even clearer. Also, keep in mind that it's okay if your goals change once in a while or become more detailed.

Everyday Things

Anything that enters your mind that makes you think; "Oh! I have to remember to...." belongs on your list! Examples:

The Short Term Plan

- Appointments
- When to pay bills
- Grocery list
- To make plans with someone important you haven't see in a long time
- By when to start something you can't do yet
- Cleaning/chores
- Oil changes
- Work hours for the week if they change

Once you have this part of your list together, you will feel less stressed. All that mental energy that you used to spend trying to keep track of things, you will get back. Anytime you might start to feel stressed, all you have to do is look at your list and work your plan!

Monthly Budget

Write down everything that you spend a month, down to the last penny. Then add it up to see how much you spend. Your first goal is to make sure how much you spend isn't more than you earn. Your second goal is to always be saving some amount every month for an emergency. Make adjustments in your spending to accomplish this. Having even just one month of bills saved up ahead can be a huge stress reliever!

Credit Histories

Having good credit in this day and age is super important. If your credit isn't doing so good, don't worry, there are always ways to get it where it needs to be. The first step is to get your credit report from the three major credit bureaus, and look up tips for building or rebuilding your credit. Freecreditreport.com is a great place to start. There are also places that offer free credit counseling if you need help making sense of it all, and most of us do! It's never too soon to get the ball rolling on this. Building credit usually takes years, and even things like work and rental history are considered when applying for credit. There are always little steps you can do right away that will make a big difference down the road.

Transportation

How well you can get around is a huge part of being able to accomplish your goals. Having a car of your own is ideal, but for some periods of time it's just not in the cards. When you are relying on buses, cabs, walking, and people giving you rides, it can be a challenge not to get frustrated.

- Use a variety of kinds of transportation so when you do get rides from people, they will know that it's for something important and super appreciated.
- If you can, try to find a job that is a central location to where you currently live, and where you think you might be likely to live in the future.
- Get familiar with stores near where you live and near your job to see how you can spend the least amount of your time and money to get the things that you need.
- Always be saving a certain amount of money on a regular basis for your car whether it's to buy a car, for an upgrade, or car repairs.

The Short Term Plan

Health

Look back at chapters 1-4 and see what fits your personal needs to add to your list. Don't overwhelm yourself, just start getting into the habit of constantly working to live and feel better mentally, physically and spiritually. Always make room on your list for taking that extra good care of yourself!

NAMING YOUR LIST

Another step to making a great to-do list is naming your to do list. It can be anything that gives you motivation every time you read it. A few ideas are:
- THE MASTER PLAN
- THINGS TO DO TO GET TO WHERE I NEED TO BE
- THINGS TO DO FOR (insert name).
- Just make sure it's not a person that might make you want to tear up your list down the road.
- (John Doe's) LIST
- You can even label it as someone else's list if privacy is a concern.
- EXCELLENT PURPLE TEDDY BEAR
  Making up a silly name for your list can keep things fun, as long as you know what it's for and it doesn't remind you of anything negative.

WORK

Work takes up a huge part of your life. Whether you're starting at the bottom or already at the top, your job can be extremely challenging to your sanity. If you're at a point where you are changing a lot of things, sometimes that requires a job change too and you might have to start at something that wouldn't be your first choice just to get going. Have a good work plan and know you won't be stuck in this job forever if you don't want to be.

You need to have a separate mind set for work and personal life. You have to remember at all times that your top reason for being there is to make money to pay your bills so that you will have more time to work your plan. Everything else comes in second.

Bosses

There isn't one boss in the world that can't be a pain from time to time. Here are some tips to make things a little easier:

- No matter what mood they are in be professional at all times. This sets a standard of how they should be acting back to you, so both you and they know what to expect on a daily basis.
- They are the boss. Period. One of the biggest complaints of bosses is that people disrespect and don't listen to them. If they are truly doing something over the line (physical assault, sexual harassment) then take the necessary courses of actions, but anything short of that, handle with a professional smile on your face.
- Take time to read your employee handbook carefully in detail. There might be a surprising thing or two to know about that you'll be glad you read later.

The Short Term Plan

- Bosses like people that make their job easier and that make them look like good bosses. Take initiative to take as much stress off them as possible, but do it in a way that makes them look good and at the same time that it makes you look good.
- Take a short class or professional workshop that will increase your job skills. (Example: if you are a cook in a restaurant, take a publically offered food safety class. Even if you may not need to, it will make you look good.)

Coworkers

At work, your goal should be to make allies, not friends. Allies know that working together will build a stronger business and make life better for both of you. Friends can take things personal and make bad business decisions that affect both of you. Conflict will happen at work, make no mistake about that. Just minimize it so that it's few and far between and not that bad when it does happen:

- Make it a point to show that you choose focusing on the work instead of the personal stuff whenever possible.
- Still be friendly and positive, just not at the expense of losing focus on your work.
- Avoid gossiping whenever and wherever possible. Listening to it is one thing, but don't chime in on it.
- Make a new rule for yourself: No complaining at work. No complaining about you coworkers, your bosses, your customers, or the actual work. Nobody likes a

whiner, and it just puts you and everyone else in a negative mood and makes the day go by harder and slower.
- Don't ask coworkers for loans or make any other agreements that there is even a small chance they could hold a grudge about later.
- Stay out of work politics. If you get into it, then you will be forced to choose a side. You want everyone to think that you are on their side. You want to be that middle ground that's as fair as possible to everyone. Being that will keep you out of A LOT of trouble.

Customers

It isn't possible to make every customer happy all the time, but this is the goal of any and every job you'll ever have. Be great with the customers and you will be making yourself just about irreplaceable:
- Remember, the most important goal to the business you work for is to make money. Your part in that is getting and keeping the customers happy and coming back again and again.
- The golden rule: Treat other people the way you would want to be treated. Most bosses understand that you can train people to work on the little details but you can't really train people how to be nice to people.
- Make a sincere connection to your customers. Make eye contact, smile and think about any extra small thing that you could say or do to make their day better.

The Short Term Plan

- Try to remember repeat customers' names. Write down the name and description of those customers and what they usually get. Study it if you need to and always keep it on you, so you can glance at it when you see them coming. Greet them by name and ask if they want their usual of____. This makes a great impression on your customers and bosses.
- No matter how good your people skills are there is always something new to learn. There are tons of great tools out there (books, articles, YouTube videos and more) to grow your verbal, body language, etc. skills.

Your goal should be to enjoy your job. The best way to do this is to be really good at it. Almost every work environment has the same things to overcome; crappy bosses, negative coworkers, difficult customers etc. But if you focus on doing a truly great job with the customers, and your daily tasks, this will keep your boss happy and you will have less mental time for your coworkers to ever become a problem. Take control, plan your work and better opportunities will come your way because good help is truly hard to find.

IMAGE

How you want others to see you is not only about how you dress and do your hair, but also about how you carry yourself. Your body language, manners, way you talk, how organized you are, and having a positive attitude are all huge things!

The Enlightened Ex-Offender

Appearance:

Is it fair that the more attractive you are the easier a lot of things are to do? No. Is this a fact of life that is likely to change anytime soon? Also no. So do what you can to make this fact work for you and not against you. And also keep in mind that the better you look the better you will feel.

- Keep your hair color and cut age appropriate. Go to a hair dresser that is a nice person, about your age, attractive and tell them what you do for a living and your goals and ask them to make you look nice.
- Dress as good as you can for your budget. You want classic pieces of cloths that you can dress up or down. You want to look "nice" more than "sexy". Don't be afraid to look in discount clothing stores. While one store might not have anything you like the next one a few miles away might have a lot.
- Small details are important. Jewelry, a lite perfume or cologne, super fresh breath, more or less makeup, or a neutral color nail polish can all go a long way.

It's What You Say and How You Say It:

Every time you speak to someone you are communicating a lot more than just words. You are telling someone how you feel about what you are saying. You are giving them an impression of what kind of person you are. Make sure you are giving them the right impression:

The Short Term Plan

- If you are talking about your goals make sure you sound excited.
- Make it a point to be as clear about what you are saying in as few words as possible.
- Leave room to let the other person talk and be a good listener. Be able to repeat back everything that was said. (Take short notes if need be).
- Always show patience with the person you are talking with.
- Your body language should agree with what you are verbally saying. Pay special attention to your facial expressions, body movement, posture, space, tone of voice, and making eye contact.

Organization

Another huge part of showing people that you have it all together is being well-organized. Having a great to do list is only the first step. There are many other ways you need to be organized. This might seem like a lot of things but they are all important!

- Time.
  - Do you make good use of your time? How much of your time is productive and how much is spent on entertainment?
  - Are you always on time? Maybe even a little bit early? Do you give yourself extra time to get to places? Always be a few minutes early

to an appointment. If you're late, people won't respect you as much.
- Neat, clean, limited clutter, with lots of open space visible. This is how you want your home, car, place of business, wallet, purse, briefcase, anything that is yours to look at all times.
- Everything should have a place it belongs (and keep it there!) The test of being truly organized is to be able to find anything quickly.
- Putting time into preparing for anything that you can see coming down the road (good or bad) is part of being organized. But keep your thoughts focused on the good!
- Writing down on a calendar the biggest most important dates as an extra reminder. (Or if you have a smartphone set reminders there too.) Even the most organized people can get so busy they forget things.
- You can try breaking your to-do list into days, weeks, months and even years. Just make sure it's something that you find easy to follow through on. Don't set yourself up for failure with too much stuff in a day, etc.
- Let go of things you don't need. Hanging on to a few things for sentimental reasons is fine, but don't let it clutter your life and therefore affect your opportunities.
- There are a lot of stores that have entire sections of things to help you get organized. Put on your

- to-do list to go browse at least once a year to update your organization.
- Have something to write with and on at all times. Just a simple piece of paper and mini pencil or pen would do, or making use of the notes app of your smartphone.
- Make sure you always have what you need for the day before you walk out the door.
- If you find yourself procrastinating on your to-do list, start with something you want to do and go from there.
- The quality of what you are getting done matters. Don't rush through the big things. Quality is in the small details.

Plan out what you need and what you think might work best. You might need to take a day just to get started organizing. In most cases becoming organized doesn't happen overnight. It's something you will have to work at to get in a routine. You may also want to experiment with different ways of organizing things. Nobody is exactly alike so different things will work for different people. Find out what works best for you!

SURROUNDING YOURSELF WELL

Who you choose to spend your time with will determine what kind of life you have. Only socialize in ways that make you a better, happier, and a more successful person. This may sound a little cold or not as much fun but give it some time and effort and you will never look back.

Some people have a greater need to be social than others. How much time you choose to spend with other people should depend on your personal needs. The more secure, happy and peaceful you are in your own skin and mind, the less time you will feel the need to spend in social settings. That being said, it's also good to be around people for community and support, just make sure it's not for negative things like superficial approval, or gossiping/talking bad of others, or as part of an addiction; alcohol, drugs, shopping, etc. If your socializing tends to get in the way of you being productive in other parts of your life decide on a certain amount of time you let yourself socialize a week, and make sure it leaves more than enough time for all the others stuff you need get done, with time left over to relax and de-stress. Remember that your social life should be part of a positive community. Surround yourself with people that either have or are working towards the same kind of things that you are. People that will bring out your best!

LIFE'S CHALLENGES

Vivian Greene said, "Life is not about waiting for the storm to pass, it is about learning to dance in the rain." There will <u>always</u> be storms. The only thing that you can count on to stay the same is the fact that everything changes. So get on your dancing shoes!

- Believe in yourself, that you can and will overcome anything that comes your way.
- Drama is a sign of not being emotionally strong. Don't feed into it, whether it's in yourself or in others.

The Short Term Plan

- Take charge of your feelings. Don't just react to things as the day goes by. Decide ahead of time that no matter what comes your way that you are going to feel positive about it. Positive attracts more positive.
- Have a space of your own you can go to and be alone with your thoughts. (Even if it's just taking a walk by yourself for 5 minutes).
- Have a plan decided of how you would handle any problem that comes at you and then put it out of your mind so that you can focus on the present good things.
- Don't settle for having ANYTHING in your life that brings you down. If you can't change the circumstance right now, change how you look at and feel about it.
- Look at setbacks as opportunities in disguise. Even if you can't see it at the time, they really always are and you will always learn something! Learn, let it go and keep moving on and up!

You should be asking yourself every day; "What am I doing today to accomplish my goals?" Getting out of your house every day, even just to run a quick errand or to the library is super important. Get out there in the right places to meet people and start building up connections that will help you accomplish your goals. There is nothing like the feeling you get from checking things off your to-do list. Be positive. Don't let any kind of negativity hold you back. Ask questions.

The Enlightened Ex-Offender

Check out things you hear about. Get out of your familiar comfortable bubble and go find opportunities. Know in your heart that you will get everything you want!

The Short Term Plan

Journal

What are five positive things about your life that you want to keep?

1. _____

2. _____

3. _____

4. _____

5. _____

What are five things about your life that you want to change?

1. _____

2. _____

3. _____

4. _____

5. _____

The Enlightened Ex-Offender

Goals
Where do you want to be in your life in a year?

_____

_____

In three years?

_____

_____

In five years?

_____

_____

Everyday Things

Start a to do list (here or on a separate piece of paper that you will carry around with you) using suggestions from this chapter topic:

_____

_____

_____

The Short Term Plan

_____

_____

_____

_____

_____

_____

Monthly Budget

Write down everything that you spend a month, down to the last penny.

_____

_____

_____

_____

_____

The Enlightened Ex-Offender

_____

_____

_____

_____

_____

How much extra do you save a month?

_____

How much do you want to be saving up a month?

_____

How will you accomplish this?

_____

Credit Histories

What is your credit score?

_____

The Short Term Plan

What are three things that you can do now to help build it for the future?

1. _____

2. _____

3. _____

Transportation

What are three things that you can do now that will make transportation easier for you in the future?

1. _____

2. _____

3. _____

Health

What are three health goals that you can start working on right now?

1. _____

2. _____

3. _____

NAMING YOUR LIST

What will you name your to do list so that it motivates you to get things done every time you look at it?

_____

WORK

What are three goals to set for what you want out of your current (or currently searching for) job?

1. _____

2. _____

3. _____

How is your mindset for work different than your mindset for your personal life?

_____

_____

What is your plan for easily dealing with your boss/bosses?

_____

_____

The Short Term Plan

What is your plan for easily dealing with your coworkers?

_____

_____

What is your plan for easily being great with customers?

_____

_____

IMAGE

What are three things that you could work on, to improve the way that people see you, and use to your advantage?

1. _____

2. _____

3. _____

Appearance

What are three things about your appearance that you would like to try different in the future?

1. _____

2. _____

3. _____

It's What You Say and How You Say It:

What are the three things under this chapter topic that would help you the most to work on?

1. _____

2. _____

3. _____

Organization

Look through all the suggestions under the organization chapter topic and choose five things that you want to add to your to do list to work on that would benefit you most:

1. _____

2. _____

The Short Term Plan

3. _____

4. _____

5. _____

SURROUNDING YOURSELF WELL

Do you need to spend more time socializing or less?

_____

Do the people that you socialize with bring out your best?

_____

LIFE'S CHALLENGES

What are your strategies for staying calm and centered when life throws you new challenges?

_____

_____

_____

The best way to keep yourself feeling good when life throws something difficult your way is to keep moving! Look back through all the journal notes from this chapter and the

The Enlightened Ex-Offender

last ones and add everything to your to-do list! Every day, no matter what is going on, look at your to-do list and pick a couple things out to work on that day. There is nothing like the feeling of knowing you're always moving forward!

The Short Term Plan

Notes:

Chapter 6

BREAKING FREE

Breaking Free from the grip of the U.S. justice system is not designed to be easy. The private prison systems make billions in profit every year. They would not make a profit if there were no prisoners to keep. The justice system is biased to look out for minorities committing crimes more than non-minorities, and the way the media presents the "average" ex-offender certainly can't be ignored as a source of the problem. This is the way the system is for now, so work within the system, as you successfully pass your way through it!

RECIDIVISM

RECIDIVISM is a word that means the re-arrest, re-conviction, or re-incarceration of former inmates. It's a big word for when the systems' rehabilitation or punishment fails to really help someone.[1] According to the Bureau of Justice Statistics; about two out of three people released from prison will be rearrested within three years. Those are not very good odds, to say the least.

What are the top reasons for recidivism?

When you read this list, don't think of it as all the reasons you are doomed. Think of it as things to be especially aware of to guarantee your success!

- AGE- The younger a person is at the time of their first arrest, the more likely that they will be arrested again.
- GENDER - males have higher arrest rates than women.
- RACE - minority groups have higher re-arrest rates.
- HISTORY OF SUBSTANCE ABUSE- The more severe the drug problem, the longer the list of arrests.
- LACK OF EDUCATION /EMPLOYMENT HISTORY - Finding a job is a requirement of probation and parole, but it is harder to find a job without much employment history and a felony on your record.
- SECURE PLACE TO LIVE - The majority of places will not rent to people with any felony on their record, making home life unstable.
- PERSONAL RELATIONSHIPS - When a person's work and home life are uncertain, personal relationships will be under more stress as a result, too.
- MINOR PAROLE AND PROBATION VIOLATIONS – A history of violating parole/probation for things that wouldn't be a crime for a regular citizen.

The Enlightened Ex-Offender

- LACK OF CONCIDERATION FROM PO'S - Parole and probation officers sometimes don't understand the difficult situations that people are in, or can't do much to help.
- PRISON BECOMING A NORMAL PART OF LIFE - So many people have either been in prison or have been directly affected that they have learned to expect and live with it as a part of their lives.[2,3]

THE MOST IMPORTANT TIME TO MAKE IT THROUGH!

Studies show that a person just let out of prison is over ten times more likely than a regular citizen to have a life ending drug overdose, cardiovascular disease, be murdered, or commit suicide in the first weeks.[4] So be careful to take extra good care of yourself during this time!

THE PUBLIC'S OPINION OF EX-OFFENDERS

Just as frustrating as being discriminated against, is realizing that many people don't care about or want to change it. The overall public opinion towards people that have committed a crime is very cold and indifferent. The media is hugely responsible for this. It is a main factor in how people form their opinions. The media is how people receive their information, whether it be through the news, TV shows, movies, advertisements, magazines, etc. The majority of stories reported about crime are the most extreme, violent, attention grabbing, shocking stories there are to cover. They do this because it keeps their ratings high so the network makes more money. The problem is that the majority of people's crimes are nowhere near that unforgiveable. It's like in grade school when the whole class gets punished because of one class clown, but instead of a pop quiz, the class gets an entire lifetime of discrimination and hardships. The Rockefeller Drug Laws are the perfect example of this. There was a mistaken belief by the public that the current laws were going too easy on the criminals, and so politicians, all too happy to please the public, passed the RDL's to get "tougher" on crime. The laws backfired and grew the problems of the justice system to whole new levels.[5]

The general public's treatment of ex-offenders is not very thought out and easily moved to anger by the media. That kind of unreasonable treatment can be a challenge to deal with. The best solution for the moment is to do the best you can with it. Patiently re-educate the people that are open to it (remember that they didn't give their permission ahead of time to be brainwashed into the way they are), and be as positive of an example as you can to break the stereotype. There is more you can do in the future but that will be discussed in chapter 8.

SUCCESSFUL PROBATION/PAROLE TIPS

1. *Figure out how the PO wants to run things*
A probation/parole officer's job is basically the same everywhere. They are in charge of protecting the public from the people they are in charge of. They are not supposed to think about their probationer first, the public's safety comes first. They are still a part of the justice system.

The Enlightened Ex-Offender

To get through probation/parole successfully, the best way is to figure out exactly what a PO wants from the people they are overseeing. They could want:

- To honestly help the people they are in charge of.
- Not to have much emotion at all and be strictly business about everything.
- Not to be bothered as much as possible.
- Fulfill a need to feel powerful or important.

It's safe to say that every PO wants respect from the start. They will usually tell people what they want in the very first meeting.

2. *Make a great first impression*
In the first couple of minutes people meet, they decide how to treat each other based on how someone looks, acts, and sounds. Here is how to make the most of those first minutes:
- Make a quick phone call to the receptionist (there is no need to say who it is that is calling), to ask if there is any kind of a dress code. For example some places do not allow shorts even if it's over 90 degrees outside.
- Be a little early. Set a time to leave by and add on extra travel time in case of delays like traffic backup from a car accident or getting stuck behind a school bus, etc.
- How someone looks means a lot. Neat and clean is the goal. Try to avoid anything too flashy or colorful.

Breaking Free

If clothing options are limited, don't worry, just make the best possible choice. Also, go light on cologne, perfume, jewelry, and makeup.
- Use "sir" or "ma'am".
- Be aware of nonverbal communication:
  - Movements and facial expressions that do not involve verbal communication.
  - Nonverbal parts of speech itself (accent, tone of voice, speed of speaking, etc.). Fast talkers should slow down a little and quiet speakers should speak up. Avoid speaking in monotone, and say words clearly.
  - Show confidence, but at the same time be respectful.
- Make meetings feel more comfortable. Change sitting and standing positions, voices and any movements to copy the PO's. Repeat their head nods and tilts. Speak at their pace and volume level. Try to do this in a natural, unobvious, simple way. This is supposed to make things feel more comfortable not weird or creepy.
- Never outshine the probation/ parole officer. Always make people in a more powerful position feel comfortably superior. In an effort to please or impress them, do not go too far in showing off any talents, or the PO could end up feeling fearful or insecure. Let them feel like the smartest person in the room.
- Ask questions to show you are paying attention to the conversation. At the same time, be careful not to ask

too many questions. This could mess up the smooth pace of the conversation, or just plain annoy the PO.
- Give clear answers to all questions. Don't avoid questions or it will look like something is being hidden. Ahead of time, think of everything that would be hard to explain and have the answer ready.
- Try not to say anything that could be taken as "they are making excuses". Be matter of fact, explain what was learned, and don't get defensive.
- Write down everything important, and keep papers in place where they can't be lost or forgotten about. The next meeting and anything that needs to be brought, done, or have gotten by then are the most important things.
- Say thank you when leaving.

3. *Understand probation officers burn-out*
When someone is suffering from burn-out, this means they are feeling tired, frustrated, or have an uncaring attitude and lack of interest resulting from stress, overwork, or intense activity over a long period of time.[6] Don't be a source of stress or frustration for a PO that has this, or they will naturally try to get rid of what stress they can, in this case, the stress being you.

4. *Distrusting government agencies*
There is a long history in America of people distrusting their government. There are very good reasons to both trust and

distrust it. Government is set up to help and protect people. Of course, there has always been the fight over which people deserve more help and protection. The problem is not the idea of government itself, but how the people in charge twist it for their own benefit. Just like anything else in the world, take time to figure out each place and person before deciding how to feel about them. Don't walk into everywhere assuming the worst. Good things can be missed if they are not being looked for.

5. *Be a master of communication*
The power to really listen to and be understood by others is a must have skill. Practice and improve the following:

- Having differences of opinion without it leading to an argument.
- To the point and clear speech.
- Understanding where other people are coming from.
- Conveying a message to others without being threatening.
- Maintaining eye contact in a conversation, with relaxed facial expressions.
- How to express feelings comfortably. Blocking emotions can lead a person to respond the wrong way in a conversation and therefore result in misunderstandings.

The Enlightened Ex-Offender

DO NOT do the following:

- Interrupt the speaker.
- Use words with completely different definitions. Words can have different meanings to different people, thus blocking communication.
- Be distracted by something that is not part of the ongoing communication.
- Get ahead of the speaker and complete his/her thoughts.
- Forget what is being discussed.
- Use negative words. Positive words get a much better reaction from people.

6. *Avoid power struggles*
The most important thing to remember about getting into a power struggle with a PO is DON'T get into a power struggle with a PO! They have all the power and the system is set up so that it can't be taken away from them. Don't fight a battle that can't be won.

7. *Inspire help*
The best way to motivate a PO to help a probationer is to make sure the PO knows about any positive change made and that the credit for that change is given to the PO. They have to feel like they are making a difference in the probationer's life. Make sure to give positive reinforcement every time they help with anything. Say for example, "Thank you. That was really a great idea." or "That book you suggested

reading really helped me to realize....". Try to keep what you say genuinely truthful.

8. *Filing a complaint against a PO*
Call a local attorney for a free consultation on the issue, but in most cases, unless there is some kind of 100% proof that a PO is in the wrong, it is not a good idea to file a complaint. The only thing that is going to change is the probationer is going to have even more problems than they did before. Try to deal with the situation in the best way possible until it's time to get off probation.

9. *Keep personal written records of everything done for probation*
Anything positive done while on probation should be written down in a notebook with a time, date, detailed description, and when possible a signature and contact information of someone who can confirm it. This could be anything from required things like community service and putting in job applications to extra things like getting a drivers license reinstated or rebuilding family relationships. Keep track of all of them in case they ever need to be proven.

10. *Try to finish the required parts of probation early*
Complete things like community service, court costs, restitution, and required classes as fast as possible. When a PO doesn't have too much to check up on for a probationer, they will not pay them as much attention. In some cases they will even let the probationer off probation early.

The Enlightened Ex-Offender

Getting all the way out of the justice systems' reach is not an easy thing to do, just remember that it can be done! Take time to really plan out the best way to move forward. Work every angle. Probation/parole may feel like it's taking forever, but that's nothing compared to the feeling of getting off of it!

Journal

What are the top reasons for recidivism?

What do you think are the three biggest challenges you face from the list in this chapter topic?

1. _____

2. _____

3. _____

What can you do to overcome them?

1. _____

2. _____

3. _____

THE PUBLIC'S OPINION OF EX-OFFENDERS

How do you feel about the public's opinion of ex-offenders?

_____

_____

_____

The Enlightened Ex-Offender

What is something positive that you can tell yourself when you get frustrated by the public's opinion?

_____

SUCCESSFUL PROBATION/PAROLE TIPS
What does your PO want?

_____

_____

_____

Where could you improve the most in "Make a great first impression"?

_____

_____

_____

Breaking Free

Where could you improve the most in "Be a master of communication"?

_____

_____

_____

How will you inspire help?

_____

_____

How/where exactly are you going to keep written records of everything you have done and will do for your PO?

_____

_____

Add anything that you need to do/positive strategies and ideas about your PO to your to-do list.

The Enlightened Ex-Offender

Notes:

Chapter 7

THE LONG TERM PLAN

Once you have solid starting goals for your life up and running you can start to think about your long term plans and goals!

EXPUNGEMENT

The first thing you need to do before you start adding to your long term to-do list is to find out if you qualify for an expungement of your record. This can get really confusing because the laws on this are different from place to place. Look in your yellow pages and find a couple local criminal lawyers that offer expungement of criminal records and call for a free consultation. If money is still a little too tight for lawyer fees, that's fine, you are just trying to get information so you know what options will be on or off the table for you in the future. Get a couple different lawyers opinions to make sure they match up. In a lot of cases you will not qualify for this, so don't be discouraged! You just want to know 100% either way so you can keep moving forward!

CAREER GOALS

What kind of work do you want to do for the rest of your life? Work takes up a large piece of your total time in life. It's a lot

easier to love what you do because you really love it instead of finding the things that you love about a job that you don't really enjoy. Doing work that you love is a very real possible thing. Start by asking yourself some questions:
- How many hours and what shifts work best for you?
- Do you enjoy working with a lot of people around, just a few, or by yourself?
- Do you like the physical, mental or both parts of a job?
- What kind of work do you find rewarding even when you are not getting paid to do it?
- Do you need to stay away from certain jobs to have a clear conscience?
- Is there a certain kind of work that drains you mentally more than others?
- How much do you absolutely need to make a week?
- Will a job allow you to have as much free time as you need?
- Is there future job security in a kind of work you like?
- Does it offer the kind of opportunity for advancement that you want?

GOING BACK TO SCHOOL

Going back to school can be a great idea, but before you sign up for anything do your research first! Look into things and ask a lot of questions to make sure that your record will not hold you back from your current goals. Many colleges and technical schools do not have the needed information about if a company will hire you after you get your degree/

certification. Call around to the human resource departments of the kind of places you would want to work for in the future to ask them how your record would affect your hiring now or in the future. Don't trust the colleges/technical schools to do this for you; it's in their best interest to paint a sunny picture to get your tuition money. Don't be or get discouraged. There are jobs out there that will fit your needs perfectly! You just have to keep looking and rethinking it out until you find it! Keep at it!

FINANCIAL GOALS

As you reach a point in your life that you are making more long term goals and plans, you have to make sure that your finances are also being updated to fit with them. Long term financial things to consider:

- Growing your savings account
- Looking into what kinds of insurance that fit your needs: Health, life, home renters, etc.
- Getting out of debt (whether it be through bankruptcy or just growing your credit score)
- Buying a big ticket item (car, house, traveling, etc.)
- Planning for retirement

HEALTH GOALS

Once you have worked on getting your mind and body right so that you can successfully move forward, keep working to make sure it stays not only at that level but that it keeps getting stronger and better for the rest of your life. What do you want to be a great example of for the people around you?

What can you work on more from chapter 2 now that you have a little more money to help improve it?

MAKING YOUR OWN SPACE

What would you do with unlimited resources to make your house more peaceful and positive? Think about it. Now take that and think about how you can accomplish those things under your budget.

- You should have lots of visual reminders that make you feel happy.
- Make use of feng shui (changing the energy of a room by rearranging the things in it).
- Add some extra security so you feel safe.
- Redecorate.
- Take down anything that reminds you of something negative and replace it with something positive.
- Make sure you **feel happy in the neighborhood you live in or consider relocation.**

GOALS CHANGE OVER TIME

You will reach many points in your life when you start to feel lost despite the fact that you are more organized and clear about your goals than ever. This is normal and healthy. As you grow and change in life so will your goals. Stop and take some time to think about where you want to go from that point.

- What do you want to change?
- What is making you happy or unhappy?
- What do you want to experience?

The Long Term Plan

Have patience. Just like your starting goals this may take some time to figure out and that is okay. Use the time you are figuring it out to observe the everyday things around you to get some ideas of what you might be searching for. Keep an open mind for what feels right to you.

Your long term goals are going to unfold over time for the rest of your life. They *are* the rest of your life. No matter what anyone else has told you, you can still live a full life with a criminal record. Knowing what it feels like to be down and out just makes everything else that comes after all the more deeply fulfilling.

Journal

EXPUNGEMENT

Do you qualify for an expungment of your record?

_____

How does this affect your future plans?

_____

_____

_____

CAREER GOALS

After reading this chapter topic, what kind of work would make you happy to do for the rest of your life?

_____

_____

_____

The Long Term Plan

How are you going to accomplish this?

_____

_____

FINANCIAL GOALS

After reading this chapter topic, what are your three biggest long term financial goals?

1. _____

2. _____

3. _____

How are you going to achieve these goals in the future?

_____

_____

_____

The Enlightened Ex-Offender

HEALTH GOALS

What are your long term health goals?

_____

_____

_____

How are you going to make them happen?

_____

_____

_____

MAKING YOUR OWN SPACE

What is your ideal of a perfect home?

_____

_____

How are you going to get it close to that in the future?

_____

_____

The Long Term Plan

GOALS CHANGE OVER TIME

How often will you re-ask yourself your goals to see how they have changed?

_____

The Enlightened Ex-Offender

Notes:

Chapter 8

Changing The System

What is happiness to you? It starts with being healthy mind, body and soul. It continues with overcoming your addictions and getting back on your feet after hard times. After you have broken free of the system that has caught you in its web and start living the kind of life that you have chosen and planned out, what's next? Is there even more?

WHY IS THE WORLD THE WAY IT IS?

The answer to this question could easily fill a thousand page book, so I will focus on the biggest part of the problem; the media!

What is the media?

The definition of media is something used to communicate and connect with people. The term mass media means that there are a very large number of people being communicated with. Here are some different kinds of mass media:
- Print Media
- Newspaper, magazines, newsletter, photography, books, leaflets, and pamphlets

- Electronic Media
- TV, radio, movies, CDs, and DVDs
- New-age Media
- Mobile phones, computers, internet, email, websites, blogging, and internet TV
- Other Types of Media: Entertainment, advertising, marketing, public speaking, and event organizing.

How much does the mass media influence people?

The average American watches more than 4 hours of TV each day. New studies show that people now spend an equal amount of time on the internet as they do watching TV.[1] The mass media is how people form their opinions about many things. It is a big part of what makes a person who they are because it strongly influences their attitudes and beliefs.

Media is a business, and a business's number one priority is to make money. The topics that make the most money are violence, sex, drama, and anything else that they think is shocking enough to grab people's attention. The average child will watch 8,000 murders on TV before finishing elementary school. By age eighteen, the average American has seen 200,000 acts of violence on TV, including 40,000 murders.[2] It's safe to say that the media is very good at making money and influencing people.

Changing The System

How does the mass media distract people from the fact that they are making the world more violent and selfish?
They accomplish this by:
- Bringing out strong feelings in people to keep them from thinking clearly.
- Encouraging all kinds of entertainment for people to care about more than they care about their day to day lives.
- Making people feel smart so they don't feel the desire to learn anything new.
- Desensitizing people so they feel uninterested in things they would otherwise have cared about.
- Limiting what is acceptable to think and talk about, but encouraging debate about what is accepted so any different opinions are labeled extreme and unacceptable to even talk about.
- Leaving out so many details about something that it's easy to twist the information to fit personal uses.
- Making up information.

Why is the news so important to keep up on?
Whether people realize it or not, everything in the news directly affects them. Caring about the news is a question of if a person cares about themselves. George Santayana said, "Those who cannot remember the past are condemned to repeat it." Some people think that it's unhealthy to watch

the news because there is always something bad on. I think it's unhealthy to avoid your problems. Face all problems with compassion instead of ignoring them with anxiety. If something is boring to watch because it's hard to understand, take time to learn about it. You should never settle for something you don't understand. Keeping up on the news makes you a better person all the way around.

The best way to get news is to watch or read a little bit of local, national, and world news on a regular basis. Take the time to figure out where the information is coming from and if it's being twisted to fit someone's personal opinion or agenda and don't be afraid to try "alternative" news sources.

Do we worry about the wrong things?

The influence of the media can leave you confused about what is important to focus on and what is not. According to Barry Glassner, the author of "The Culture of Fear: Why Americans Are Afraid of the Wrong Things", we have to learn to recognize when a fear is not really as big of a threat as it is being made out to be. The problem is that there is a lot of money being made off of tricking people into worrying about the wrong things. A ton of products are being sold and studies being done, for things that should be at the bottom of the worry list. As a result, things that need to be worked on, like poverty for example aren't getting enough attention. We really are destroying ourselves by worrying about the wrong things. Just remember that knowledge helps control fear.[3]

THE REAL PROBLEMS

The biggest problems in our society today not only affect the ex-offender community, they affect everyone, especially the more vulnerable parts of the population. (Which includes ex-offenders)

Homelessness

According to the National Alliance to End Homelessness, there are 633,782 people experiencing homelessness on any given night in the United States.

Mental Health

The most recent numbers say that there are over 60 million visits to physician offices, hospitals as an outpatient, or emergency rooms with a mental disorder as the primary diagnosis a year in the US.[4]

Poverty

Half of Americans live below or near the poverty line.[5] The Census Bureau says that the percentage of people in poverty in the US is 15%. But they don't give you the whole picture and fail to mention how many are so close that they are getting the same affects.

Greed

Some people think that greed is good, that it gets things done. But exactly what is getting done? It does earn people a lot of money, usually hurting other people in some way. Greed is about fearing the future, the fear of not having enough. Greed should be viewed as the negative that it is, instead of a normal accepted way of life.

Inequality

Inequality is measured by how big the gap is between rich people and the poor people. The more unequal a country's people are to each other, the more unstable its economy is. The United States ranks the highest of all the industrialized countries for inequality and the divide is getting bigger every year.[6] The following things are more problematic in unequal countries:

- Health
- Levels of trust
- Mental illnesses
- Drug use
- Life expectancy
- Infant mortality
- Obesity rates
- Educational access
- Teen births
- Homicide rates
- Children experiencing conflict
- Rates of imprisonment
- Social mobility
- Recycling
- Innovation
- Violence
- Equal opportunities for everyone

Changing The System

- Equality in politics
- Social justice
- Economic efficiency[7]

Why is the issue of inequality such an emotionally filled topic?

No one (rich or poor) likes to be called a bad person or be morally judged by another person. With great money comes great power. Material things (other than the basic necessities in life) aren't the real issue. Its power that's the real issue. Focus on what people are doing with their power!

Food and Agricultural Issues

They include topics such as Global Food Crisis's, Food Aid, World Hunger, Causes of Hunger as Related to Poverty, Food Aid as Dumping, Obesity, Sugar, Beef, Tobacco, Genetically Engineered Food, and many more.[8]

Loss of Biodiversity and Extinctions

These include massive extinctions from human activity, declining amphibian populations, loss of forests, misuse of land and resources and more.[9]

Suicide

More people die by committing suicide every year than by any other type of violence including armed conflict, and 20 times more people attempt it and don't succeed.[10]

These topics are only the tip of the iceberg. There are many many more just as important issues that need to be addressed by US as citizens of this world.

WHAT CAN YOU DO ABOUT IT?

To really be free in this world you have to feel like the world is going to get better. Being aware of and understanding a problem is the first step on the journey to making it better. The second is to start making little changes with yourself.

Be self-educated

Self-education is when someone teaches themself new skills, knowledge, wisdom, theories, concepts or subjects that make their life better. You can teach *yourself* what you need to know to get to a better place in life.[11] Anyone who knows this fact has a huge advantage over other people. The more self-education and therefore knowledge you have, the harder it is for another person to get over on you.

What is the Most Important Thing to Learn About?

Anything you don't fully understand, that directly effects your life, is a great place to start self-educating. Two perfect examples of this are government and politics. The mention of these two words almost never fails to get a giant yawn reaction, I know, but suck it up! These are the two biggest things people are getting scammed by because they don't understand them! There are sources to learn this information from out there that won't put people to sleep. A person

Changing The System

just has to look until they find something that will work for them. Also, keep track of what has been learned and more ideas of what to learn about by writing it down in a journal or notebook. Doing this gives a greatly deserved sense of accomplishment and self-esteem every time you looked at it.

Don't Have a Lot of Free Time or Money at the Moment?

Almost everyone these days doesn't have a lot of extra time. This is why a decision has to be made every day, to find a way to fit in time for self-education. Set up an amount of time every day to start out with that will be dedicated to this. Even starting out with just five or ten minutes a day is okay. Make it "bathroom reading time" if necessary. As time goes on a person will find that the more they learn, the more they have a strong desire to keep learning.

Don't have the money to spend at an expensive book store? Libraries offer free services that should more than fit anyone's self-education needs. There are also many people that have books lying around their house that might be perfect to borrow. It's a lot easier to find someone willing to loan out a book than someone willing to loan out money to buy a new one.

Self-Help Books vs. Shrinks

Self-help books tell readers how to overcome different personal problems.[11] They are a lot cheaper than psychologists for common problems. If there is a serious mental issue like bipolar disorder, schizophrenia, or that sort of thing, go to a doctor. But if it's more like struggling with communication in a relationship or tips for organizing a part of life better, save some time and money and grab a self-help book on that subject. Look around the self-help section in a local book store or library to get familiar with all the different topics that are covered. It's also important to pay close attention to how a book makes you feel when reading it. It should feel positive, and empowering.

Learn New Technologies Whenever Possible

Technology is constantly changing. It's all too easy to fall behind in understanding how it all works. Learning new technologies is something that will pay off, and create another personal advantage for someone's entire lifetime. Technology can be expensive, especially new technology. It's probably not going to be possible to just buy all the newest stuff, like computer programs and phones for example, and learn by just playing around with them. When you come across a technology that you're not familiar with, start out by Googling it to get the basics of how it works. It's better to at least have a basic understanding of something than to have no idea at all. Just like learning anything else, technology may be frustrating at first, but learning a little at a time will prevent one big splitting headache in the future!

Activism

The definition of activism is the use of direct action to achieve an end, either for or against an issue.[12] It's the

getting out there and doing something about what you want to change.
- Protesting to try to get laws changed
- Signing a petition
- Not buying or consuming certain products
- Building up your community
- Spreading the word on an issue that's important to you

You can make activism a daily part of your life. It feels great to know you really are doing something every day that will truly make a difference. Make a plan and start today!

Networking

You can't know everything by yourself, that's what networking is for. The definition of networking is a supportive system of sharing information and services among individuals and groups having a common interest.[13] In other words, get to know everyone you meet to see if there is anything that they can help you with or that you can help them with to further your goals. Don't bore people with your life story when you first meet but briefly share what you're about and find out what their interests are. It won't take long to find out if you can be helpful to each other or not. Be genuine and a good listener. Use in person contact and over the phone, computer etc. Keep good organized records of who you meet, how they could be helpful and their contact info. With practice you will be an expert networker in no time!

The Enlightened Ex-Offender

THE BEAUTIFUL TRUTH

We are all connected
When you help others, you are helping yourself
When you help yourself, you are helping others

Changing The System

Journal

WHY IS THE WORLD THE WAY IT IS?
What role does the media play in your life?

_____

_____

How much TV do you watch a day?

_____

What are three ways that you can reduce the medias effect on your thoughts and life?

1. _____

2. _____

3. _____

Where will you get your news from?

_____

_____

The Enlightened Ex-Offender

What things do you worry about that are actually minor?

_____

_____

WHY IS THE WORLD THE WAY IT IS?

How do/ have each of the following problems affected you or somebody you care about?

Homelessness

_____

_____

Mental Health

_____

_____

Poverty

_____

_____

Changing The System

Greed

_____

_____

Inequality

_____

_____

Food and Agricultural Issues

_____

_____

Loss of Biodiversity and Extinctions

_____

_____

Suicide

_____

_____

The Enlightened Ex-Offender

WHAT CAN YOU DO ABOUT IT?

You have to let yourself see, think about and remember the good things that happen and that people do for each other in this world. Every day find and write down at least one thing. What did you find today?

_____

_____

What are three things that you would like to teach yourself?

1. _____

2. _____

3. _____

What are three things that you don't understand that you would like to?

1. _____

2. _____

3. _____

Changing The System

How are you going to teach yourself these things?

_____

_____

What new (or new to you) technologies would you like to learn?

_____

_____

What are three ways that you can use activism to change things you care about?

1. _____

2. _____

3. _____

The Enlightened Ex-Offender

What are three ways you can be a good networker in the future?

1. _____

2. _____

3. _____

Add the things above to your to do list!

Changing The System

Notes:

APPENDIX

Classes/Meetings Using The Enlightened Ex-offender Book

One Meeting

One meeting can be used to introduce people to the book and give a sense of community and hope.

Two Meetings

The first meeting would be the same as the above one meeting with a follow up class to talk about everyone's thoughts after they have read the book.

Nine Classes

The first Class is to introduce the book and talk about the first chapter. The "homework" of this class would be to complete the journal at the end of the chapter. Classes two through eight are to talk about the journaling from the last chapter and then to introduce the next chapter (completing the journal at the end of the chapter before the next class). The ninth class (after chapter eight journaling is discussed) is to talk about what everyone thought about the book and their plans for the future.

What's Said Here Stays Here Policy

At the start of every meeting/class there should be a reminder that what is said in the meeting/class is not to be repeated unless permission is given, so people will feel more free to talk, etc.

*If you are on probation or parole check with your PO to make sure that attending a class/meeting with other ex-offenders does not violate any conditions of your probation/parole.

Appendix

The Enlightened Ex-Offender Completion Form

Reader's Name _____
Date you finished this _____
Did you like this book? Why or why not?

_____

_____

_____

_____

Would you suggest to someone to read this book? Why or why not?

_____

_____

_____

Write a brief summary of your thoughts on this book:

_____

_____

_____

The Enlightened Ex-Offender

_____

_____

_____

_____

_____
Signature of reader _____

ABOUT THE AUTHOR

Corey Austin is an ex-offender dedicated to helping other ex-offenders successfully rebuild their lives as she has. Ms. Austin was born and raised in Toledo Ohio, a city influenced heavily by the surrounding major cities of Detroit, Cleveland and Chicago. Starting at the age of 20 years old she acquired a "tour" of the justice system in county jails, state prison, probation departments, and homeless shelters.

The Founder of The Enlightened Ex-Offender, Corey can be reached at:

Email: coreyaustin@ymail.com
Website: Theenlightenedex-offender.com
Facebook: The Enlightened Ex-offender
Twitter: Corey Austin @ EnlightenedExO

Chapter Notes

Chapter 2

[1] The American Journal of Clinical Nutrition, American Journal of Clinical Nutrition, Vol. 77, No. 2, 288-291, February 2003,© 2003 American Society for Clinical Nutrition, Will there be a tipping point in medical nutrition education?

[2] Sage journals online, Personality and Social Psychology Bulletin, Breaking Habits With Implementation Intentions: A Test of Underlying Processes, Marieke A. Adriaanse Utrecht University, Utrecht, Netherlands, M.A.Adriaanse@uu.nlHYPERLINK "/search?author1=Peter+M.+Gollwitzer&sortspec=date&submit=Submit"Peter M. Gollwitzer New York University, New York, NY, USA, University of Konstanz, Konstanz, Germany, Denise T. D. De Ridder Utrecht University, Utrecht, Netherlands, John B. F. de Wit Utrecht University, Utrecht, Netherlands, University of New South Wales, Sydney, Australia, Floor M. Kroese Utrecht University, Utrecht, Netherlands, Published online before print February 11, 2011, doi: 10.1177/0146167211399102 Pers Soc Psychol Bull April 2011 vol. 37 no. 4 502-513, date accessed 6/3/11, http://psp.sagepub.com/content/37/4/502.short

[3] Discovery Fit and health, Is it true that if you do anything for three weeks it will become a habit? by Julia Layton,

Habits: Make It and Break It, Copyright © 2011 Discovery Communications, LLC. The number-one nonfiction media company. date accessed 6/12/11, http://health.howstuffworks.com/mental-health/human-nature/behavior/form-a-habit3.htm

[4] Alvarez, G. G. and Ayas, N. T. (2004), The Impact of Daily Sleep Duration on Health: A Review of the Literature. Progress in Cardiovascular Nursing, 19: 56–59. doi: 10.1111/j.0889-7204.2004.02422.x(date accessed 6/3/2011)

[5] The Mayo Clinic, Health Information, Adult Health, 10 Tips For Better Sleeping, by Mayo Clinic Staff, July 7,2009, date accessed, 6/3/11http://www.mayoclinic.com/health/sleep/HQ01387

[6] BBC Health, treatments, Fluids, Dr Toni Steer, BBC 2011, date accessed 6/4/11, http://www.bbc.co.uk/health/treatments/healthy_living/nutrition/healthy_water.shtml

[7] Centers for Disease Control and Prevention, Nutrition for Everyone, Water: Meeting Your Daily Fluid Needs, Page last reviewed: February 23, 2011, Page last updated: February 23, 2011, Content source: <u>Division of Nutrition, Physical Activity and Obesity,</u> <u>National Center for Chronic Disease Prevention and Health Promotion</u>, date accessed 6/4/11, http://www.cdc.gov/nutrition/everyone/basics/water.html

Chapter Notes

[8] The True Power of Water, Healing and Discovering Ourselves, Masaru Emoto, Atria Books, Beyond Words Publishing, 2005.

[9] Health Discovery, a Weight Watcher Support Network, Why is Exercise Important?, Armand Tecco, M.Ed. January, 1999, date accessed 6/13/11, http://www.healthdiscovery.net/articles/exercise_importa.htm

[10] The Mayo Clinic, Health Information, Fitness programs: 5 steps to getting started, By the Mayo Clinic Staff, December 18, 2010, date accessed 6/13/2011, http://www.mayoclinic.com/health/fitness/HQ00171.

[11] FOX16.com, Is "Detoxing" Your Body Safe?, reported by Justin Earley, Updated 11/17/08, published 11,16,08, date accessed 6/28/11, http://www.fox16.com/news/local/story/Is-Detoxing-your-body-safe/Jproh7Bi0EajAZRw1Dw4fg.cspx

[12] Health.com, How to Detox Your Body, Twelve ways to remove and avoid toxins in your home and in your body, Chris Woolston, Last Updated: March 15, 2009, date accessed 6/28/11, http://www.health.com/health/article/0,,20411560_1,00.html

[13] MSN Health, Diseases & Conditions, What Your Body Says about your health, By Sally Wadyka for MSN Health & Fitness Medically Reviewed by: Farrokh Sohrabi, M.D. I

February 23, 2011, date accessed 7/2/11, http://health.msn.com/health-topics/what-your-body-says-about-your-health

[14] The Wall Street Journal, Health Journal, U.S. Edition home, What Your Body is Telling You, Article, By MELINDA BECK, Printed in The Wall Street Journal, page D1, 6/23/09, date accessed 7/2/11, http://online.wsj.com/article/SB124571709339739367.html

[15] Urban Institute Research of records, publications Health and Prisoner Reentry
How Physical, Mental, and Substance Abuse Conditions Shape the Process of
Reintegration, Kamala, <u>Christy Visher</u>
Publication Date: February 15, 2008date accessed 7/5/11, Permanent Link: http://www.urban.org/url.cfm?ID=411617

Chapter 4

[1] http://medical-dictionary.thefreedictionary.com/addiction

Chapter 6

[1] Definitions are from Dictionary.com/ Reference.com.

[2] Bailey, Kristen. "The Causes of Recidivism in the Criminal Justice System and Why It Is Worth the Cost to Address Them." Nashville Bar Journal. Dec 06/Jan 07. (April 21, 2009).

Chapter Notes

3   Connecticut General Assembly, Office of Program Review and Investigations, "Recidivism in Connecticut", study from 2001.

4   Ingrid A. Binswanger, M.D., Marc F. Stern, M.D., Richard A. Deyo, M.D., Patrick J. Heagerty, Ph.D., Allen Cheadle, Ph.D., Joann G. Elmore, M.D., and Thomas D. Koepsell, M.D., "Release from Prison — A High Risk of Death for Former Inmates" (N Engl J Med 2007; 356:157-165January 11, 2007).

5   Ernest Drucker, Population Impact of Mass Incarceration Under New York's Rockefeller Drug
Laws: an Analysis of Years of Life Lost, (Journal of Urban Health: Bulletin of the New York Academy of Medicine Vol.79, No. 3 September 2002, © 2002 The New York Academy of Medicine).

Chapter 8

1   Kristina Knight, "Study finds TV time, Online time equal", BizReport: Research: January 04, 2011,
http://www.bizreport.com/2011/01/study-finds-tv-time-online-time-equal.html#.

2   http://www.csun.edu/science/health/docs/tv&health.html

3   Barry Glassner, The Culture of Fear (Basic Books: a member of the Perseus Books Group, 1999) xv.

4 Taken from CDC main website

5 http://www.salon.com/2013/05/30/half_of_americans_living_below_or_near_poverty_line_partner/

6 Anup Shah, Poverty Around The World, Global issues, Social, Political, Economic and Environmental Issues That Affect Us All, This Page Last Updated Sunday, January 02, 2011, http://www.globalissues.org/article/4/poverty-around-the-world#InequalityinIndustrializedNations.

7 Global Issues, Social, Political, Economic and Environmental Issues That Affect Us All, Issues on the Global Issues web site, © Copyright 1998–2011. http://www.globalissues.org/article/4/poverty-around-the-world#Introduction

8 Global Issues, Social, Political, Economic and Environmental Issues That Affect Us All, Issues on the Global Issues web site, © Copyright 1998–2011, http://www.globalissues.org/issue/749/food-and-agriculture-issues.

9 Global Issues, Social, Political, Economic and Environmental Issues That Affect Us All, Issues on the Global Issues web site, © Copyright 1998–2011, http://www.globalissues.org/article/171/loss-of-biodiversity-and-extinctions.

10 More people die from suicide annually than from violent acts – UN health official, UN News Centre, 10 September

Chapter Notes

2009, http://www.un.org/apps/news/story.asp?NewsID=32016&Cr=mental+health&Cr1.

[11] By Bulliongrey, eHow Member, How to Self-Educate in Any Subject, Copyright © 1999-2011 eHow, Inc, http://www.ehow.com/how_5473557_self-educate-subject.html.

[12] http://www.yourdictionary.com/activism

[13] http://dictionary.reference.com/browse/networking

www.ingramcontent.com/pod-product-compliance
Lightning Source LLC
Chambersburg PA
CBHW050642160426
43194CB00010B/1776